10/92

D0603409

Don't Sing Before Breakfast, Don't Sleep in the Moonlight

Don't Sing Before Breakfast, Don't Sleep in the Moonlight

Everyday Superstitions and
How They Began

by Lila Perl

illustrated by Erika Weihs

Clarion Books
New York

To Erika Weihs, with appreciation

Clarion Books
a Houghton Mifflin Company imprint
215 Park Avenue South, New York, NY 10003
Text copyright © 1988 by Lila Perl
Illustrations copyright © 1988 by Erika Weihs

Library of Congress Cataloging-in-Publication Data
Perl, Lila.
Don't sing before breakfast, don't sleep in the moonlight.
Bibliography: p.
Includes index.
Summary: Examines common superstitions associated
with the events of a typical day, how these supersti-
tions developed, and how they influence our behavior
today.
1. Superstition—Juvenile literature.
[1. Superstition]   I. Weihs, Erika, ill.   II. Title.
III. Title: Do not sing before breakfast, do not
sleep in the moonlight.
BF1775.P33 1988   001.9′6   87-24295
ISBN 0-89919-504-0

HAL   10 9 8 7 6 5 4 3

Contents

Superstition tells us not to sing before breakfast because it's too early in the day to be happy.

Don't Sing Before Breakfast

If you sing before seven,
You'll cry before eleven.

If you sing before you eat,
You'll cry before you sleep.

You wake up on a bright winter's morning. It's January and supposed to be very cold this time of year where you live. But there's a "January thaw" taking place, a kind of "false spring." A bar of golden sunlight stripes the wall opposite your bed. Small birds are twittering gaily in the leafless trees outside your window.

The balmy air, the glowing morning, the happy sounds, all make you feel wonderful. You throw off the covers and leap out of bed, *singing* . . .

STOP! You're making a terrible mistake. In fact, you may already have made several serious errors in starting the day. You have not obeyed certain unwritten laws of the ages. As a result you may have called monster-size forces of evil into play.

We are talking, of course, about superstition. If you have

ever seen anybody knock on wood, cross fingers, skip over a crack in the sidewalk, or toss some salt over one shoulder, you have watched superstition in practice.

Many superstitious acts — like being careful not to sing before breakfast — seem very silly on the surface. Do they have a deeper meaning? How did they start? Why have people kept them up?

The very word *superstition* means ideas or practices that "stand over" or "above" us, that "survive" in spite of reason and logic. Some superstitions go back almost to the very beginnings of human life on Earth. Whenever they began, in the darkened past, the reasons for them at the time seemed very sound.

According to what we know today, there is no scientific basis for most superstitions. Yet they continue to be passed on from one generation to another. And almost all of us cling to a few of them.

One reason for holding on to superstitions may be simply force of habit. Another reason may be the realization that science has not yet come up with all the answers. Magic still fires our imaginations. We figure that it doesn't hurt to take a few small precautions, carry a charm, or make a wish, just to be *sure* that good luck rather than bad follows us around from day to day.

So we "don't sing before breakfast." Why? Because it is just too early in the day to be happy. According to old beliefs, happiness had to be earned each day. Only a fool would sing — or laugh — before doing some useful chores or accomplishing a satisfactory piece of work. Otherwise bad luck, always ready to pounce, would see to it that sadness or tears followed, surely before the day was out and probably even sooner.

If you sing before seven, you'll cry before eleven, so the old rhyme goes.

It's very likely that all of us can remember a day when early-morning gaiety was followed by weeping. So maybe — just maybe — there is some truth to this superstition after all.

Did you know that even getting out of bed can be dangerous if it is not done correctly? When people are cross and ill-tempered, we say they must have "gotten out on the *wrong* side of the bed" that morning. Or we say that they started the day "on the wrong foot."

Like the "wrong" side of the bed, the "wrong" foot is the left one. "Best foot forward" always means the right foot.

Getting out on the right side of the bed and putting on your right shoe first is said to start the day off well.

The ancient Romans were so worried about visitors entering their houses with the left foot instead of the right that they stationed a servant called a "footman" at the door to keep watch.

Superstition tells us that right is better than left because most people are right-handed. They have more power and grace in their right hands. From earliest times, people who were born left-handed were looked upon with fear and distrust. Their movements seemed clumsy, awkward, and "unnatural." They were believed by some to be insane, to have criminal tendencies, or — worst of all — to be possessed by the devil. *Sinister*, meaning "evil" or "ill-omened," comes from the Latin word that among the ancient Romans meant "left." And the French word for "left," *gauche*, has come directly into English as another way of saying "awkward."

We know today that none of these terrible suspicions about left-handed people are correct. Favoring one hand over the other probably has to do with the messages sent by the two halves of the brain. Most people get the "message" to be right-handed. But if left-handed people were the majority, the right hand would almost certainly be the "wrong" hand.

Even so, we still watch anxiously to see if a baby will reach for a toy or a cup with the right hand or the left. And some of us are very careful to step off the *right* side of the bed with our *right* foot, and to put on our *right* sock and our *right* shoe first.

Many hotel and motel rooms, in fact, are designed with beds arranged so that no wall will interfere with a sleeper getting out on the right side of the bed.

Here are some more "right side, left side" superstitions:

Right ear itching — someone is saying something nice about you

Left ear itching — someone is speaking ill about you

Right eye itching — you're going to have a pleasant surprise

Left eye itching — you're going to have a disappointment

Right palm itching — you have money coming your way

Left palm itching — you will have to pay out money

Itchy feet, though, both right and left, mean you are soon going on a journey. And an itchy nose means that you are probably going to have a quarrel. Since itching makes us feel irritable, there may be more than a little truth to that superstition.

*

As we all tend to be a little fuzzy-headed in the morning, we may behave rather absentmindedly. For example, we may put some of our clothing on inside out. This happens to be very lucky, provided we do it by accident *and* we don't notice our mistake for most of the day.

This superstition stems from the old-time belief that death was able to recognize you by your garments. To wear them inside out confused evil spirits and turned them away. It was also once believed that a woman who was having mishaps in the kitchen could reverse her ill fortune by turning her apron to the opposite side. The evil spirits causing her cooking to curdle, burn, or boil over would no longer know her and would scamper off. Similarly, a workman who was dropping his tools or hammering his thumbs might turn his cap front to back to change his luck.

Yawning, something we are also apt to do early in the morning, can be dangerous. People once believed that yawning was caused by the devil, whose favorite way of jumping into the body was through the mouth. So, even though we may be all by ourselves when we yawn, superstition tells us to cover our mouths. This may not be a bad idea, as it's also good practice for when we yawn in front of others.

Sneezing is another hazardous act. It was once thought that the breath was the soul. When people died, their souls were said to leave their bodies. And, of course, the dead no longer breathed. It was feared that the breath *and* the soul could escape the body, even by means of a sneeze. This is why almost every language has a saying that means "God bless you" or "health" to protect the sneezer.

On the other hand, sneezing on demand became quite the fashion in Europe in the 1600s. Men inhaled a pinch of ground-up tobacco, called "snuff," through the nostrils to bring on a hearty sneeze that was said to clear the head. They sneezed at almost everything throughout their conversations. Only matters of the highest importance were "not to be sneezed at." Supposedly, they all kept their bodies and souls together by constantly wishing one another *"Gesundheit!"*

There are many superstitions about the meaning of sneezes. Three in a row are good luck, for three is a lucky number. But a sneeze under a wedding canopy may mean that the "soul" will go out of the marriage and it will not last.

There is even an old rhyme that tells us which days are safe for sneezing and which are not:

Sneeze on Monday, sneeze for danger;
Sneeze on Tuesday, kiss a stranger;
Sneeze on Wednesday, get a letter;
Sneeze on Thursday, something better;
Sneeze on Friday, sneeze for sorrow;
Sneeze on Saturday, see your true love tomorrow.
Sneeze on Sunday, your safety seek,
Or the devil will have you the rest of the week.

Hiccuping, like most of the sneezing we do, seems to come on for no reason at all. Down through the ages, hiccups were a source of mystery. Naturally, they were blamed on the devil. Victims were said to be possessed, for there were some cases where hiccuping went on for days and even a few that were said to have led to death from sheer exhaustion.

We know today that hiccups have to do with the diaphragm and other organs in the chest. But, interestingly, some of the old folk remedies for curing hiccups still work. One of them tells us to drink a glass of water and then recite these words three times while holding our breath:

As I went over the bridge,
The hiccups fell in the water.

Another trick is to drink nine gulps of water without taking a breath. In the old days, people probably thought these cures worked, because they used the so-called magic numbers of three and nine. The truth is that the counting times in these remedies forced one to hold one's breath long enough for air to be pushed through the proper passages and so stop the hiccups.

Like singing or laughing early in the day, whistling in a

house is said to invite bad luck. But to whistle at sea is even more dangerous. This is because the sound of whistling resembles the wind. It has been said that if a sailor or a visitor aboard a sailing ship should whistle carelessly, he or she can bring on a storm.

Women were often considered bad luck on ships. This was partly due to the fear that they might be witches. Women were also unfairly judged because they were sometimes ignorant of the superstitions of the sea. A captain's daughter who once whistled at sea is said to have given rise to the verse that tells us:

> A whistling girl and a crowing hen,
> Always come to no good end.

On the other hand, a very soft, careful sailor's whistle may be helpful in "whistling up a wind" when a sailing ship is becalmed.

Two places, though, where one must never whistle are down in a mine or in the dressing room of a theater. The first could cause a cave-in and the second a bad performance that might "bring down" the house with whistles, boos, and catcalls. This would lead, of course, to the play closing and to the actors being unemployed.

Some dog owners snap their fingers when whistling for their dogs. The snapping is supposed to break any spells being cast by evil spirits answering to the whistling. In general, whistling isn't thought to bring very good results. The expression "You can whistle for it" means you probably won't get what you want.

*

Whistling may bring bad luck, so some dog owners snap their fingers to drive off evil spirits.

Cutting your fingernails is something you may find yourself doing when you are getting ready to start the day. As there are a number of superstitions about nail-cutting, it might be best to think first about what day it is and then consult the following rhyme:

> Cut your nails on Monday, cut them for wealth;
> Cut them on Tuesday, cut them for health;
> Cut them on Wednesday, cut them for news;
> Cut them on Thursday, a new pair of shoes;
> Cut them on Friday, cut them for woe;
> Cut them on Saturday, a journey to go.
> Cut them on Sunday, cut them for evil,
> For all the next week you'll be ruled by the devil.

Witches are said to gather nail trimmings, so we pick a lucky day for cutting and never leave trimmings lying about.

On whichever day you cut your nails, you should be very careful not to leave the trimmings around for evil spirits to get hold of. It is best, according to an old superstition, to bury them under an ash tree, or some other tree believed by the ancients to be sacred. In some superstitious families, it is the custom for mothers to bite rather than cut their babies' fingernails during the first year of life. For even a sliver of cut fingernail that falls to the ground might end up in the hands of a witch.

Witches and sorcerers, it is said, can cast powerful spells using nail trimmings or hair clippings or even threads from the garments of those they wish to harm. They may fashion miniature figures of their victims out of wax or clay, add the discarded nails or hair, and then chant a fearsome curse. They may also stick pins into various parts of a figurine in order to inflict pain or injury on the person it represents.

Hair has long been thought to be connected in some way with a person's life force or inner strength. In the biblical story of Samson and Delilah, the hero Samson was robbed of his tremendous physical power when Delilah cut his hair as he slept.

To this day, many people feel that if you give a lock of your hair to another, such as a loved one, you are placing yourself in that person's power. And parents who clip a child's baby curls for a keepsake must guard them very carefully.

Like nail cuttings, hair clippings should never be carelessly tossed away. It is best to burn hair so that not a trace will remain for a witch to find. A special danger is supposed to arise from shaking hair clippings out into the garden. If a bird should make a nest from a person's hair, it is said that the person will suffer headaches until the nest falls apart.

Now that you have carefully observed some of the early-morning superstitions such as getting out on the *right* side of the bed and *never* singing before breakfast, you are ready to try your luck in the world beyond your front door.

Just keep in mind that, although black cats and sidewalk cracks await you, there is always wood to knock on, a rabbit's foot to carry, even — if fortune really smiles on you — an iron horseshoe lying in the road.

As cracks in the pavement are thought to represent the openings to a grave, we try very hard to avoid them.

Don't Step on a Crack

Step on a crack,
Break your mother's back.

Step in a hole,
Break your mother's sugar bowl.

Have you ever walked along the sidewalk being very careful not to step on the cracks in the paving? Perhaps the old rhyme above came to mind. Experts who study folklore and folk sayings think that the "crack" represents an opening in the earth that leads to a grave. The "hole" is the grave itself.

Nobody really knows why stepping on a crack should bring bad luck to one's mother rather than some other person. Even worse, the broken back is often interpreted to mean death. And the broken sugar bowl is definitely a bad omen.

From quite early times, it was the custom of some peoples to bury their dead with articles of crockery. But first they would "kill" the "spirit" that lived in the bowl or plate. They did so either by driving an opening through its center or smashing the entire piece to bits. This ancient practice may well be the reason for the connection between a "hole," or grave, and a broken sugar bowl.

Most of us, of course, don't believe in the superstitious rhyme about avoiding cracks and holes. If it were true, we would all become motherless orphans at a very tender age. Similarly, we say that if we step on an ant, it will rain (possibly as a punishment for having killed an innocent creature). But if every ant or beetle crushed underfoot caused even a drizzle, the Earth would have been flooded eons ago.

One of the real hazards of trying to avoid cracks, holes, and crawling insects when we venture forth is that we may stumble.

Stumbling or tripping is supposed to be a dangerous sign. Stumbling as we leave the house is said to be caused by evil spirits who live on our doorstep. Some people think it is a warning not to go any farther. We can try, though, to change our luck by doing and saying the following:

> I turn myself three times about,
> And thus I put bad luck to rout.

That *should* take care of the demons lurking in our doorways. But not always. One reason given for the old custom of the groom carrying his bride across the threshold of their new home is to keep her from tripping. Such an accident would invite bad luck at the very start of their life together. No one, though, ever seems to have given a thought as to what might happen if the heavily burdened groom were to trip!

Sometimes another reason is offered for the bride's being carried over the threshold. It goes way back to the days of

The groom carries the bride into her new home because evil spirits lurking on the doorstep may cause her to trip.

"bride capture," when a wife-to-be was stolen from an enemy and carried into the cave or hut of her captor. She was his property from then on.

When it comes to stumbling, theater people are probably the most superstitious of all. Some actors believe that to trip as one walks onto the stage is lucky because it gets the evil happening out of the way. Others say it is a bad sign that will be followed by the actor's missing a cue or forgetting a line.

But stage people never disagree about the danger of wishing one another "good luck" just before they face an audience. They feel these words are a sure invitation for mischievous forces to do their worst. So instead, they say just the opposite: "Break a leg." In the German theater, especially at the opera, performers go a step further. As they are about to set foot on the stage, they tell one another, *"Hals und Beinbruch,"* or "Break your neck *and* legs!"

In recent times there has been a new theory about stumbling. Human-behavior specialists say it is caused by something in ourselves that does not *want* to go forward. So, if you stumble out of the house some morning on your way to school or work, don't blame the wicked sprites on your doorstep. Your mind may be simply telling your body that it wishes it would go back to bed.

*

Once you *are* out and about, you may encounter even more hazards — for instance, a tall ladder leaning against the side of a building. Few of us will boldly walk under a ladder, for we've always heard that this is bad luck. But why? There is, naturally, the danger that a can of paint, a heavy tool, or some other object may fall on our heads. But there's a less obvious reason for this superstition.

In and of themselves, ladders are considered lucky symbols. The ancient Egyptians often placed small ladders in the tombs of their loved ones to help the souls of the dead "climb" heavenward in the afterlife. But a leaning ladder, or even an open stepladder, that forms a triangle with the ground is another matter. The three sides are said to represent the basic family unit, the very means by which life goes on. In the Christian faith, Joseph, Mary, and Jesus are called the "holy family." The much older religion of ancient Egypt had several holy families composed of father, mother, and child. Probably the best known was that of the god Osiris, the goddess Isis, and their son Horus.

So, walking under a ladder is said to bring bad luck because passing through the triangle violates the unity of the family. However, if you should unthinkingly find yourself under a ladder, you can still try to save yourself by crossing your fingers or by spitting three times between the rungs. On the other hand, if you decide to go *around* the ladder, be careful when walking out into the traffic. You don't want to invite some other calamity!

On a really "unlucky" day, you might not only stumble over your doorstep and walk under a ladder, but a black cat might also cross your path.

Cats were not always thought to be unlucky. The ancient Egyptians worshiped the cat and even had a goddess named Bast who was the patroness of cats. It's quite easy to understand the Egyptian fondness for cats. They were not only house pets, they also hunted and killed the rats and mice that would otherwise have overrun the storehouses in which

The danger of being hit by a falling object is only one of the reasons we are warned not to walk under a ladder.

the Egyptians kept their grain. Cats were often honored in ancient Egypt by being mummified after they died. Thus their bodies were preserved just like those of Egypt's kings and other important people.

In parts of Europe, however, by the time of the Middle Ages, people began to believe that witches could change themselves into cats. So the black cat became a spooky symbol of Halloween. And all black cats came to be feared as witches in disguise!

There are many myths about cats that have probably led to our thinking of them as supernatural creatures. It isn't true, though, that cats can see in complete darkness or that they have nine lives. They do, however, have good coordination and a flexible spine, so they are less likely to hurt themselves in falls and other accidents.

There doesn't seem to be much we can do to counteract the bad omen of seeing a black cat. But it may be a comfort to know that in England black cats are considered lucky, and *white* cats are feared. Some people think this is because of the mummified cats that British archeologists found in ancient Egyptian tombs and brought back to England. All of the "lucky" Egyptian cats were black, as a result of the drying-out process used to make mummies. This left the British with only white cats to worry about!

*

Certain objects that we are likely to handle almost every day, both inside and outside our houses, are also said to have the power to bring us bad luck. Who hasn't heard that breaking a mirror can lead to seven years of misfortune?

Although breakable glass mirrors probably weren't widely

known until around the 1300s, people have long feared having their image shattered. The very first "mirrors" were quiet pools of water. People looked into them, saw their reflection, and believed they were seeing their soul, or life force. If an enemy came by and threw a stone in the pool, the reflection broke up. This meant an evil fate was in store. If the soul was taken away completely, the person would die.

With the increased use of glass mirrors, many new superstitions came along. Some people believed that all mirrors had to be covered in a house where a death had taken place. Otherwise, the soul of the dead person might be caught in the mirror and would not find its way to heaven. A different reason for covering the mirrors was to prevent the mourners from seeing their haggard and tear-stained faces. If they did, they might be tempted to stop weeping for their dead before the mourning period was up.

Some say that a baby should never be held up to a mirror during the first year of its life. Infancy is a time of great danger and the child's soul might be captured by the angel of death or by an evil spirit. The worst fear of all among superstitious people is that they will look into a mirror and not see any reflection at all. This is a sure sign that death is very near.

What about the "seven years of bad luck" said to follow the breaking of a mirror? This superstition probably has something to do with the so-called magical properties of the number seven. One long-held belief is that the cells of the body renew themselves completely every seven years. So, at the end of that period, we are not the same person we were at the beginning. Therefore, we cannot be affected any longer by the "curse" of the broken mirror.

Unfortunately, there is no truth to the seven-year theory

about our body cells. There may be another explanation, though, for the penalty we are said to pay for breaking a mirror. When glass mirrors first appeared they were so costly that it might well have taken seven years to save enough money to replace a broken one!

*

It's probably not an exaggeration to say that really superstitious people are afraid of their own shadows. Just as they fear having their reflection shattered, they believe they can be harmed if somebody walks on their shadow. They also

We can be harmed if someone walks across our shadow, so say some superstitious folk.

23

say that if they should shiver or shudder for no apparent reason it means that somebody is walking on the spot where their grave will be.

With these and so many other bad omens said to threaten us, we can all use some good-luck charms to help us get through the day.

One of the best known is a rabbit's foot. It certainly doesn't hurt, we feel, to keep one in our pocket on the way to school or work on the day of a big test, a job interview, or some other momentous happening. Actors like to keep a rabbit's foot in their dressing room or even on stage with them, hidden in their costume. Many gamblers carry a rabbit's foot. And a mother may tuck one into her baby's carriage before an outing.

But what makes a rabbit's foot lucky, and why do we often hear that the charm must be a hind foot? The answer seems to have two parts. First, rabbits breed rapidly; they can have a number of litters in a year and therefore many offspring. At one time, when most tasks were performed by human labor, having lots of children was considered a sign of wealth. So people looked to the rabbit as a symbol of prosperity and plenty.

As to the hind foot of the rabbit, this is the part of the body with which it burrows underground. People often feared the unknown depths beneath the Earth's surface. The rabbit's ability to live in a burrow and give birth to its many young there seemed proof of its power to overcome evil.

Another lucky charm is a four-leaf clover. Three is usually considered a luckier number than four. But since clover is a plant that ordinarily has three leaves, it's the unusual four-leaf specimen that is prized. The four leaves are said to stand

The luckiest of all four-leaf clovers is the kind you discover for yourself in a garden or field.

for the arms of the cross. Long before Christianity, the cross was a powerful symbol. A pair of crossed sticks was used to make fire. And the four ends of the cross pointed in the four directions of the compass — north, south, east, and west.

Nowadays, plant breeders have learned to grow four-leaf clovers. Sometimes they are encased in plastic and offered for sale. So almost anyone can own such a charm. But many people feel that the kind you find by accident while picking your way through a field of clover is the best. Even if you don't find a four-leaf plant, you will still have spent a little time "in clover," an expression that means being in a state of happiness and well-being.

A type of clover known as the "shamrock" is the national flower of Ireland. It is said to have been planted there by Saint Patrick and is considered lucky because its three leaves represent the Holy Trinity of the Christian faith — the Father, the Son, and the Holy Spirit. Probably the only thing luckier than the three-leaf shamrock is a four-leaf shamrock.

The kinds of luck bestowed by a four-leaf clover are described in this popular verse:

> One leaf for fame, one leaf for wealth,
> One leaf for a faithful lover,
> And one leaf to bring glorious health —
> Are all in a four-leaf clover.

Lacking a four-leaf clover or some other token of fortune, we can make a good-luck sign for ourselves simply by crossing our fingers. The cross is said to "trap" evil at the point where the two arms meet. Do you ever find yourself crossing your fingers while wishing very hard for something? What you are really doing is making sure that any bad luck hovering about is firmly caught and won't spoil your wish.

Another good-luck sign we make with our fingers is the circle. By bringing our thumb and forefinger together, we form a ring. This shape is said to have two meanings, both of them good. As a circle has no beginning and no end, it is a sign of everlasting life. At the same time, a circle or ring is believed to enclose luck.

Spitting on our hands is yet another way of ensuring our good fortune. Long ago, people observed animals licking their wounds and decided that saliva had curative powers. It does seem a natural instinct among humans, too, to bring an injured finger to the mouth to soothe it.

The belief in saliva as a magical fluid has led to all sorts of spitting practices. We may spit on our hands before throwing a pair of dice, before picking up a baseball bat, before a fight, or before starting to dig or perform some other physical task. What we are really asking for is a bit of added luck or strength.

Spitting is also believed to be a way of keeping wicked spirits away after a fright or other threat to our well-being. And, just as when we spit through the rungs of a ladder, it is always best to do so three times. For three is said to be one of the luckiest of numbers.

*

When it comes to seeking out good luck by knocking on wood, there doesn't seem to be any limit to the number of times that it's best to do it. But why do we "touch wood" or rap our knuckles on it in the first place? This superstition goes back to the early days when people believed that the spirits of the gods lived in trees. Perhaps the idea started with the god of lightning. When lightning struck a tree, it meant that the god's powerful magic had entered it.

So, when we are speaking of some good fortune that has come our way — or even boasting a little — we knock on the nearest piece of wood. We are asking the god-spirit inside the wood to see that our luck stays with us. Or, as the saying goes:

Wedding rings are meant to stand for both a long marriage and one filled with happiness. These circlets of romantic love are worn on the fourth finger of the left hand because of an ancient Egyptian belief that a vein in that finger runs directly to the heart.

A ring worn through the ear is also supposed to bring luck. Old-time sailors often wore an earring through one earlobe to protect them from the dangers of the sea. The piercing of the lobe was supposed to release any harmful spirits that might inhabit the body. The ring that was then inserted was intended to bring long life.

There is no truth to the belief that having one's ears pierced will improve one's eyesight. Yet some parents have been known to pierce a child's ears and insert earrings for that very reason. Perhaps this practice is connected with the myth that sailors were able to see long distances at sea *because* they wore a ring in one ear.

An earring in the shape of a circle is said to bring good luck at sea, sharp eyesight, and a long life.

> Touch wood,
> It's sure to come good.

If we knock very loudly, we may be accomplishing something else as well. The noise may keep those ever-listening forces of evil from hearing of our good luck in the first place!

If wood is lucky, iron may be even luckier. The discovery of iron, in rocks and other natural sources, and of methods for working it into tools and weapons, changed civilization. Many people felt that iron was endowed with magic. Then, in the tenth century, an English archbishop named Saint Dunstan was said to have put the devil to flight with an iron horseshoe.

Although of noble birth, Saint Dunstan worked as a blacksmith in his youth. One day, as the story goes, a two-legged creature with hoofs came to the blacksmith's forge and asked to be shod. Saint Dunstan recognized this creature as the devil and drove the nails into his feet with such force that the devil howled in pain. Before he fled, he promised never to enter a house with a horseshoe over the door.

Ever since, people have felt that a horseshoe is a good-luck object. Some say this is because many horseshoes used to have seven nails; others say it is because the horseshoe is in the shape of the new moon, which is a symbol of good fortune; and still others say it is because the horseshoe is made of iron. Nor does everyone agree about whether to nail the horseshoe over the doorway with the points facing up or down. Most people seem to believe the horseshoe's points should be uppermost, because otherwise the luck could drain out from the bottom. Those who argue for the opposite say that the points can suck in the devil from below

A horseshoe lying in the road is sure to prove a lucky find, especially if it has seven nail holes in it.

should he try to enter the house. Whichever way we hang our horseshoe, the most important thing is to nail it in securely. An iron horseshoe that falls on someone's head is never lucky!

Like the four-leaf clover you find in a field, the best kind of horseshoe is the one you find lying in the road. In the age of automobiles, though, such a find would truly be a rarity.

The anti-evil qualities of iron seem to apply even to iron nails, which are said to be a good way of testing for witches. If a nail is hammered into the footprint of a real witch, she will return and pull it out. A suspect who is innocent will continue on her way. Nails were sometimes driven into babies' cradles, and even into the beds in which childbirth took place, to prevent a witch from harming the newly born infant.

Bent nails and even bent pins are considered lucky. Perhaps this is because they resemble a horseshoe in shape. There is an ongoing disagreement about whether a pin lying with its point toward you should be picked up or not. Some people insist this is dangerous and repeat the old saying: "Pick up pins, pick up sorrow."

But the majority seem to feel that it is lucky to pick up all pins, just as the well-known rhyme advises:

> See a pin,
> And pick it up,
> All the day,
> You'll have good luck.
>
> See a pin,
> And let it lie,
> You'll want a pin,
> Before you die.

After a morning's outing filled with dangers you've just barely warded off with charms and lucky finds, it's probably time to break for lunch. But, if you are superstitious, this doesn't mean that you can relax. Before you sit down, be very careful to count the number of people at the table. And, above all, don't spill the salt!

Spilling some salt over your left shoulder is supposed to drive off any evil threat-ening this once-precious substance.

Don't Spill the Salt

Pass me salt,
Pass me sorrow.

Spill the salt,
And trouble borrow.

Tossing a few grains of spilled salt over one's shoulder is among the oldest of all superstitions. If you've ever seen anybody do this — or have done it yourself — you may have stopped to wonder what this almost automatic gesture is all about.

Still another rhyme tells us:

> If the salt thou chance to spill,
> Token sure of coming ill.

But what makes the spilling of salt so terrible in the first place?

Since very early times, salt has been prized for its seemingly magical properties. To start with, human and animal life couldn't exist without salt. Salt makes up nearly one per cent of the human body. We can actually taste it in our blood, sweat, and tears.

We connect salt with sorrow because tears are salty. It is, in fact, a Jewish funeral custom to serve a meal of salty foods after a burial. This is said to help the mourners replace the salt lost in the tears shed at the graveside.

Among the many amazing qualities of salt are its wide-ranging uses as a preservative, and not only in foods. The ancient Egyptians used salt, gathered from desert oases, to dry out the bodies of the dead and transform them into long-lasting mummies.

Salt can melt ice and snow, and at the same time it can help to freeze ice cream. It is also a cleanser and a mild antiseptic, useful for killing germs and drawing out impurities. But most of all, it is a basic part of our diet.

Early peoples watched animals travel long distances to salt licks — rocks or soils with a high salt content. They themselves worried about a scarcity of salt. In ancient Rome, salt was so valuable that soldiers and laborers sometimes received part of their wages in lumps of salt, which in Latin is *sal*. The wages were called *salarium*. Our word "salary" comes from this Latin word.

The value placed on salt helps us to see why accidentally spilling it was once considered a serious matter. It seemed to some people that an evil power was threatening our supply of this precious substance. Like all evil, it was lurking just to the left of us. So it became the custom to pick up a few spilled grains with our right hand and quickly toss them over our left shoulder. The tossed grains were a bribe to the bad spirits, urging them to be on their way.

Salt is also a symbol of everlastingness because it does not decay. And, of course, it means wealth because of its connection with "salary," or the earning of income. So it is often brought as a token of good luck to the occupants of a new house, along with other gifts such as a loaf of bread (for plenty to eat), a candle (for light), and a lump of coal (for warmth).

There are a number of well-known expressions having to do with salt. When we say that someone is "the salt of the earth," we mean that that person is truly praiseworthy. But, on the other hand, to say that someone is "not worth his salt," tells us that he (or she) doesn't amount to much. Lastly, to take something "with a grain of salt" means not to trust the "sweetness," or the truth, in what we hear. The sharp taste of a single salt grain is sure to jolt our senses awake.

Rice is another food believed to have magical powers. It is thought to bring prosperity and plenty. So, long ago it became the custom to shower a newly married couple with rice following the wedding ceremony.

The original idea behind throwing rice at newlyweds was to symbolize the hope that they would have many children. In lands where rice was the staple, people wanted large families to help grow this basic food. The tossing of other grains, like wheat and barley, has also stood for fruitfulness in a marriage. And the ancient Romans are said to have thrown nuts at the bride and groom.

Later it became an Italian custom to give almonds covered with a hard, white sugar coating to wedding guests as souvenirs. And nowadays, instead of throwing rice, wheat, or barley, tiny bits of colored paper known as "confetti" may be tossed at the happy couple, almost anywhere in the world. The name *confetti* comes directly from the Italian word for

Showering the bride and groom with rice is another way of wishing them health, wealth, and many children.

"confections," or candies. But the meaning behind the showering of confetti — just as in the case of rice — is for a happy and fulfilling marriage.

As grains are a sign of bounty, the bread baked from them is a symbol of warmth and friendship. It is believed that people who have "broken bread" together will always remain devoted to one another. The "breaking" of bread goes back to the days when loaves were about the size of large rolls and so were broken rather than sliced.

Another superstition stems from the fact that bread that has been buttered can never be "unbuttered." If two people walking side by side are temporarily separated by another person or by some object, they must immediately say "bread and butter." This will guarantee that nothing will ever part them permanently.

As for a slice of buttered bread that is dropped on the ground buttered-side-down, this is *always* considered to be bad luck — which of course it is!

*

Have you ever been urged to eat fish because it is "brain food"? Sometime during the nineteenth century, it was discovered that fish was rich in the chemical element phosphorus. And it was known that the human brain also contains a lot of phosphorus. So it seemed logical that fish would "feed" the brain. The more fish you ate, the smarter you'd be.

Actually there's no direct connection between the fish on your plate and the phosphorus in your brain. Fish, of course, is generally nutritious, but eating more of it won't help you pass a test in calculus.

What about poultry? Why do we place so much faith in

A secret wish, we say, will be granted to the one who breaks off the longer end of the wishbone.

the wishbone of a chicken, turkey, goose, or duck? We believe that if two people make secret wishes while holding onto the ends of the bone, the person who breaks off the longer end will see his or her wish come true.

This superstition takes us back to ancient times when the crowing of a cock was said to foretell the future. After all, every rooster seemed to know when a new day was about to dawn. So perhaps these barnyard animals also had some hidden knowledge of the fate that awaited their human masters.

Often, roosters and chickens were slaughtered in sacrifices to the gods. Their insides were then carefully studied for messages from those mysterious far-off spirits. After the other remains were disposed of, the wishbone — which is really the collarbone — would be saved and dried. Its resemblance in shape to a horseshoe may have added to the belief in its mysterious power to keep evil away and to grant wishes.

Even a food such as the onion is thought to tell us something of what the future holds, as in the verse that says:

> Onion's skin, very thin,
> Mild winter coming in.
> Onion's skin, thick and tough,
> Coming winter, cold and rough.

There is little proof that onions are first-rate weather forecasters. There is no question, though, that onions can make us cry. When an onion is cut, its strong oil gives off an odor that stings the nerves in our nose that connect with our eyes. Soon tears begin to flow.

Because of the powerful smell of most varieties of onions, some people believe that they can combat both poisons and germs. Old remedies include putting cut onions on bee stings and snake bites. Onions placed on the chest are also said to be able to cure colds and lung infections. And a warm, roasted onion held against the ear is supposed to ease an earache.

Some of our faith in the magical powers of the onion may come from the ancient Egyptians, who saw the onion as a symbol of eternity. This is because it is made up of layers of globe-shaped skins, one enclosing the other, and each in the never-ending form of a circle.

Garlic may be even mightier than the onion in its ability to cure our ills. A clove of garlic, cut open and placed on an aching tooth, is said to relieve the pain. The truth, however, may be that the taste and odor will be so overpowering that all our other senses will be dulled. Some people recommend that raw garlic be eaten in the spring to "purify" the blood after a winter in which it has grown "sluggish." And others say eating lots of garlic "oils" the joints and is therefore effective against rheumatism.

Another superstition tells us that even the *sight* of a ropy garland made of garlic bulbs, hung across the doorway of a house, will keep evil spirits at a distance. And before the days of inoculation against childhood diseases, many children wore pouches hung from cords around their necks. The pouches contained garlic, camphor, or other strong-smelling substances. Unfortunately, these weren't the least bit helpful in fighting off the deadly germs of disease.

"An apple a day keeps the doctor away." Here is another food that is said to bring us good health. In a different version of this popular saying, we are told:

> Eat an apple before going to bed,
> And you'll make the doctor beg his bread.

Apples have a long history in which they are linked with health, love, and death. They may even be the forbidden fruit that caused Adam and Eve to be cast out of the Garden of Eden. However, the Bible does not mention the apple specifically — only "the fruit of the tree." And nobody is certain that any apples — with the possible exception of small, sour, untempting ones — grew in the Holy Land in biblical times.

Forbidden fruit or not, some people do believe that Adam got a piece of the apple stuck in his throat. And that's why the bulge that men have in the front of the neck is called the "Adam's apple." Actually, this movable knob is a bit of cartilage, or soft bone, on the outer part of the larynx, or voice box. Women, too, have an Adam's apple. But it is usually less noticeable, partly because it is smaller and partly because it is concealed by a fleshier covering.

When it comes to love, an apple is said to be helpful in revealing the name of the person one is to marry. First, pare an apple round and round in one long, unbroken piece. Then, as the apple is said to send evil spirits fleeing, toss the paring over your left shoulder. The shape it forms on the ground will be the initial of the first name of your future wife or husband.

To find out the *order* in which a group of young people will marry, each must tie an apple to a string and twirl it over a hot fire. The person whose apple falls first will marry first, and so on. As to the "apple of one's eye," that is, of course, one's favorite and most special person.

In some countries, it is an old custom to plant an apple or other fruit tree upon the birth of a child. As the tree grows and prospers, so will the child. But beware of an apple tree

An apple tree planted upon the birth of a child is said to ensure that both will thrive, prosper, and be fruitful.

that mysteriously puts forth blossoms in the autumn, especially if fruit still hangs from the tree. This unnatural-seeming growth is thought to be the work of the evil one. Those who follow this superstition believe that someone in the family will soon die. There is even an old verse to bear out this prophecy:

> A bloom on the tree,
> When the apples are ripe,
> Is a sure termination,
> Of somebody's life.

Grapes are considered a good-luck food, probably because they grow in clusters and so are a sure sign of plenty. It's a custom in some Spanish-speaking countries to eat twelve grapes at each of the twelve strokes of midnight on New Year's Eve. This is said to ensure prosperity in the new year. If there are no grapes to be had, raisins — which are dried grapes — will do. Grapes are also thought to possess a magical quality because they can be transformed into wine — sometimes called the "blood of the grape" — through the natural process of fermentation.

We've probably all heard the childhood myth that swallowing grape pits, watermelon seeds, or other fruit pits can cause appendicitis. Actually, an inflammation of the appendix is caused by an infection. So even if you swallow a few pits as you are gulping your twelve New Year's Eve grapes, you can still hope for a very good year.

*

A food that seems to have captured everybody's imagination is the egg. It is a symbol of fertility because it brings forth life. And it represents immortality because the life it produces — the chick — will go on to produce more eggs. An egg with a double yolk is considered twice as lucky as an ordinary egg. Some people believe that eating one will bring about the birth of twins. This may be lucky or not, depending on how large a family one wants!

The Easter egg is associated with Jesus Christ's miraculous rebirth after death. And its bright decorations show our joy in the flowering of spring. But did you know that for some superstitious people the egg has a dark side, too?

Never, we are told, leave an empty eggshell faceup in an eggcup. It can become a "witches' ferryboat," inhabited by evil fairies who can do all manner of damage. They can even go to sea and cause shipwrecks. So empty shells must be turned upside-down, or be thoroughly smashed.

"You can't make an omelet without breaking eggs," the saying goes. But please be sure to beat the eggs in a clockwise direction as if you were following a southerly route from east to west. Then you will be tracing the daily path the sun takes as seen from Earth. In beating cream or stirring cake batter, we are also advised to work with a clockwise movement. Otherwise, the superstition warns us, the cream will curdle and the cake will not rise.

This caution is believed to have originated with the sun worshipers of olden times. If you think you can bake a successful cake by beating the batter counter-clockwise, try it sometime and see. Who knows? Maybe you can!

As a meal draws to a close, we are told never to help ourselves to the last piece on the serving platter. To do so means that we won't marry, or that if we are married, we may soon find ourselves single again. This myth may have been dreamed up to enforce some old-fashioned rule of etiquette.

Actually, there is nothing wrong with taking the last offering on the platter if all others have declined it. In fact, it's a compliment to the cook.

Lastly, a food superstition popular at either mealtime or teatime concerns the "reading" of tea leaves. Some people claim to be able to tell fortunes from the patterns the leaves form in the emptied teacup.

The usual method is to swirl the leaves and last drops of liquid three times. Then turn the cup upside-down onto the saucer. The leaves in the saucer will reveal the past; the leaves remaining in the cup will foretell the future. Remember, of course, that using a tea bag or a strainer in preparing the tea won't do. The tea must be drunk with the leaves floating around in it like seaweed.

An important rule to observe when we have finished eating is to place our dining utensils on our plate alongside each other, or parallel. To cross our knife and fork is believed to be dangerous. Some say this is because the form of

To foretell the future, we try to "read" the pattern of the tea leaves that are left in the cup.

the cross should not be imitated by two pieces of unwashed cutlery. As a practical matter, pieces that are crisscrossed are more likely to fall off the plates as they are being removed from the table!

Whether clean or dirty, a dropped knife is supposed to foretell that a man is about to visit. A dropped fork usually stands for a woman, and a teaspoon for a child or unmarried girl.

Because a knife has a sharp cutting edge, it is considered bad luck to give anyone even a tiny penknife as a gift. A knife, scissors, or other sharp or pointy instrument will "cut" the friendship or love that exists between two people.

The way to get around this problem is to ask for a small coin in return. This means that the knife or scissors has been "bought" rather than accepted as a gift. Incidentally, if one suspects that witches are invading one's home, an emergency remedy is to open a pair of scissors into the shape of a cross and place it on the doorstep. Be very careful, though, not to forget it's there. Tripping or falling on a scissors could be very bad luck indeed!

Have you ever wondered if there is any connection between a spoon and spooning? "Spooning" is an old-fashioned term for a show of affection between a young, unmarried couple — and yes, there's a connection. It used to be the custom in Wales, which is part of Great Britain, for a young man to give a hand-carved wooden spoon to the girl he was going to marry. The lovers' initials would be carved on the spoon. In a way, the spoon became a symbol of their engagement. Perhaps this is why the spoon has come to stand for an unmarried girl.

Finally, as you rise from the table, you might take a last look around to make sure there weren't thirteen of you seated there. People who fear the number thirteen believe that one person of the thirteen is sure to die within the year. There is even a name for this "number" fear. It is called "triskai-dekaphobia" and comes from the Greek. The word is made up of the syllables *tris* (three), *kai* (and), *deka* (ten), and *phobia* (fear), or "three-plus-ten fear."

There are at least two famous meals of the distant past that led, we are told, to a death as a result of thirteen people being gathered at table. One is the Last Supper, at which the guests were Jesus Christ and his twelve followers, or disciples. One of the disciples betrayed Jesus, who died on the cross the following day.

Another source of the superstition about thirteen at table comes from the Scandinavian, or Norse, myth that tells of

A superstitious guest will try to avoid being the thirteenth at the table.

the death of the god Balder. This young god of brightness and beauty attended a feast with twelve other gods and goddesses. Among them was Loki, the god of mischief, who hated Balder. He plotted to have Balder's brother hurl a dart of mistletoe at him and so brought about the death of the best loved of all the Norse gods.

Happily, there are lucky numbers as well as the fearsome thirteen. Some of the most favorable, in fact, are said to be the uneven numbers under ten. Referring to the number three, Shakespeare wrote in his play *The Merry Wives of Windsor*, "I hope good luck lies in odd numbers." As we can all use a few more good-luck charms as we go through our day, we couldn't agree more!

Lucky indeed are those of us upon whom the Three Graces have bestowed their gifts of joy, beauty, and wisdom.

Never Two Without Three

Never will come to thee,
Two without three.

As for three on a match . . .
This never must be.

The hree is one of those uneven numbers under ten that is usually thought to be lucky. It is the number of the basic family unit of mother, father, and child, through which life renews itself. So we often say that good things such as gifts, letters, and visitors come in threes. In other words we are "three times lucky."

Almost everybody has heard of the Three Graces, sister goddesses of Greek mythology who bestowed joy, beauty, and wisdom on humans. There are also the Three Kings, wise men of the East, who brought rich gifts to the infant Jesus. And, of course, there are the three virtues — faith, hope, and charity.

A great many other things seem to come in groups of three. We divide time into past, present, and future; and each day into morning, noon, and night. We say that the world is made up of three "kingdoms" — animal, vegetable, and mineral. And there are three primary colors — red, yellow, and blue — that are the source of all other colors. In uttering charms and spells, we often say them three times to be sure their magic will work.

But there is another side to the number three that we need to be wary of. If good things can come in threes, so can bad things like accidents, breakages, and deaths. And who can forget that in baseball it's three strikes and you're out!

Some people believe that there is a way to lessen the bad luck connected with having three things break in a row. If you accidentally break a cup or a plate, immediately break two more pieces of crockery, choosing the oldest, most chipped pieces you can find. This will prevent something valuable being broken as the prophecy fulfills itself.

What about the "three on a match" superstition? How did it start, and why is it so dangerous?

Since matches weren't even invented until the 1800s, this is a fairly recent superstition. It is believed to have started in the Boer War, which was fought in South Africa from 1899 to 1902, and to have become even better known during World War I, which took place in Europe between 1914 and 1918. Both these wars were fought from trenches, ditches cut into the earth from which the armies defended themselves. It was said that if three soldiers in a trench tried to light their cigarettes from one match on a dark night, the enemy would have just enough time to spot them and train their guns on them. The last flicker of the match, as the third cigarette was lit, could be the signal that would spell death for all.

Nobody knows for sure if anybody ever really was shot

for this reason in wartime. Perhaps all that happened was that here and there a soldier's fingers got singed as the match he held burned low. This superstition, in fact, is said to be traceable to a man named Ivar Kreuger, who had been born in Sweden and who controlled the world's supply of matches in the early 1900s. He was known as the "Swedish match king" and was anxious for his business to continue to prosper. So it's not unlikely that *he* started the "three on a match" rumor in order to sell more matches!

Although we can see that the number three may have its risky side, odd numbers are still thought to be luckier than even ones. No one knows when this idea began. But it goes back at least to the time of the ancient Roman poet Vergil who wrote, "In an uneven number, heaven delights."

*

The uneven number one is certainly considered luckier than two when it comes to paper money in the United States. So many people are suspicious of two-dollar bills that bank tellers find they are often not accepted, or are turned in for two singles.

One reason may have to do with the rules that were set up for betting at horse races. According to law in the United States, the smallest amount one could bet was two dollars. There were a great many such small bets, and naturally there were more losers than winners. People decided that two-dollar bills were unlucky, and soon nobody wanted one in his or her wallet.

If you should find yourself stuck with a two-dollar bill, it's believed that you can take the "bad luck" out of it by carefully turning down one corner in the shape of a small triangle. The triangle's sides add up to the number three, which can act as a charm against the bill's "evil." Another reason, of course, why so many people shake their heads at two-dollar bills is that they're afraid they'll get them mixed up with their one-dollar bills and give them away by mistake!

The number two also seems unwelcome in a deck of cards. The two of hearts, diamonds, clubs, or spades is usually the card with the lowest value in the deck. Many players refer to it as the "deuce," which is an old-time word for the devil.

Another even-numbered card that is considered unlucky is the four of clubs. It is also known as the "devil's bed-stead." This is because the four black, clover-leaf shaped clubs on the card resemble the knobs of a four-poster bed.

Cardplayers, who are often very superstitious, sometimes try to change their luck when they are losing. One way to do this is to get up from the table and spin one's chair around

Two, being the card of lowest value in the deck, is often shunned as unlucky by card players.

Four, though an "unlucky" even number, is connected with several good-luck symbols; our five fingers, five toes, and five senses, as well as the five-pointed star, make five one of the favored odd numbers.

three times before sitting down again. Another is to walk around the table three times. Or players may try turning their chair completely around in the hope that this will "turn" their luck. They will then sit facing the table with legs astride the *back* of the chair.

In spite of four being an even number, most people do not find it to be especially unlucky. In addition to the four directions of the compass — north, south, east, and west — there is the good luck associated with the crossed sticks that are the symbol of fire-making, with the cross of Christianity, and with the famed four-leaf clover. We also say that there are four elements — earth, air, fire, and water. And, best of all, the number four combines with the lucky number three to give us the luckiest of all numbers — seven.

But before we get to seven, what about five and six? Five, being an odd number, is thought to be lucky. And we are lucky, of course, to have five fingers and five toes. We also speak of the five senses, which are sight, hearing, touch, smell, and taste.

The five-pointed star is said to be based on the human figure of a head, two arms, and two legs. Stars of this design appear on the United States flag, one for each state. Five-pointed stars are also often awarded as symbols of merit. We've all heard of three-star restaurants, four-star movies, and five-star generals. So stars of this shape can bring good luck indeed.

What about the six-pointed star? This kind is made up of two triangles, the first resting on its base and the second resting on its point, one imposed on the other. In the Star of David, the ancient symbol of Judaism, the triangles are usually interlaced. This star appears on the flag of the country of Israel.

Although six is an even number, it doesn't seem to be particularly unlucky. Perhaps it is just a little lackluster. The British coin known as a "sixpence" isn't very much money. And six of anything is, after all, only half a dozen.

On the other hand, we sometimes hear of a "sixth sense." This is a kind of mysterious power of knowing, or foretelling, that doesn't seem to come from any of our five senses. It appears to be magical in origin. Having a sixth sense may, in fact, cause people to suspect us of being in touch with the world of the supernatural.

*

Have you ever been in "seventh heaven"? This is one way of describing a state of supreme joy. It is the way we feel when good fortune has smiled on us and we are extremely happy and fulfilled. The only thing better than heaven is a "seventh" heaven.

From ancient times, people were convinced that no number was luckier than seven. This was because there were

The seven heavenly bodies convinced the ancients that seven was the luckiest of numbers. (1) Sun, (2) Mercury, (3) Venus, (4) the Earth's moon, (5) Mars, (6) Jupiter, and (7) Saturn.

seven heavenly bodies that clearly appeared in the day and nighttime skies. They were the sun, the moon, and the five planets closest to Earth. The seven-day week arose from this enchantment with the number seven. The human life span was divided into "seven ages," from infancy to old age. And the waters of the world were designated the "seven seas." From the time of the ancient Greeks, it became a popular pastime to make lists of the "seven wonders of the world," both human-built and natural.

It has long been believed that to be a seventh son of a seventh son, or a seventh daughter of a seventh daughter, endows one with special powers — those of healing and of being able to see the future. However, with families growing smaller in most parts of the world, the likelihood of inheriting a seventh child's gifts does appear to be shrinking.

But we still attach magical powers to the number seven in all sorts of ways. Which of us, for example, hasn't stood up at a baseball game for a "seventh-inning stretch"? Aside from stretching to relieve tension and the dull ache from sitting too long, the idea of standing at the seventh inning is to bestow good luck on the home team for the remaining innings!

Back in the less lucky world of even numbers, and moving from baseball to the game of pool, we often hear the phrase "behind the eight ball." But what exactly does this expression mean?

One of the ways in which pool is played is by dividing fourteen of its fifteen balls between two players. One player has to hit the balls numbered one through seven into the pool-table pocket; the other has to sink the balls numbered nine through fifteen. The eight ball must always be pocketed last.

Often, however, the eight ball will lie on the table in the direct path of one of the other balls. A player who accidentally hits it into the pocket before the other balls are played automatically loses the game. So, finding ourselves "behind the eight ball" is really another way of saying that we are in an uncomfortable, perplexing, and risky situation.

Even kisses that add up to the number eight are not all that lucky. The following verses are from a poem called "Rory O'More or Good Omens," written in 1826 by Samuel Lover:

> "Now, Rory, leave off sir; you'll hug me no more;
> That's eight times today that you've kissed me before."
>
> "Then here goes another," says he, "to make sure,
> For there's luck in odd numbers," says Rory O'More.

Nine is the last of the odd numbers under ten. Unlike the others, it has the special feature of being divisible by a number other than itself. It can be divided by the lucky number three, for it is made up of *three* times that number. We say that cats have nine lives because they seem to emerge unharmed from deathly escapades over and over again. We say that somebody is "dressed to the nines," meaning to the highest possible degree. And we speak of a "nine-days' wonder," referring to someone who has gained tremendous, although short-lived, success.

Have you ever heard of a ninety-nine-year lease? When some valuable piece of land or other property is being leased for such a long time, why not round it off at one hundred years? Those of us who've been examining number superstitions know the answer. Nine is lucky, and ninety-nine is doubly so, while one hundred is an "unlucky" even number.

*

There are some people who would even argue that, in spite of all the triskaidekaphobes in the world, thirteen belongs among the lucky odd numbers. Back in the 1880s a group of British journalists got together and formed the *London Thirteen Club*. Their purpose was to prove that the widespread fear of the number thirteen was a lot of nonsense.

The club would meet on the thirteenth day of the month, sit down to dinner with thirteen at the table, spill the salt, and so on. Its members even made a point of wearing peacock feathers in their buttonholes. The round, eye-like spots on the feathers had always been connected with the "evil eye" by superstitious people.

The club members would also bring their umbrellas along and open them indoors. This has always been considered bad luck. Some people say that it is a way of inviting rain — and other unfortunate events — into a house because it shows "disrespect" for the protective roof that is already there.

The fates of the members of the *London Thirteen Club* are unknown, which is quite a good sign. If anything terrible had happened to them, we probably would have heard about it.

In 1946, a *National Committee of Thirteen Against Superstition, Prejudice, and Fear* was organized in the United States. Its founder was a motion-picture executive named Nick Matsoukas. His name had thirteen letters in it, and he was the thirteenth child in his family. He had been born in Greece on June 13 and arrived in the United States on February 13, 1917.

The day he founded his committee was a Friday the thir-

Anti-superstition societies set out to prove that there was nothing to fear from such threats as the "evil eye," a black cat, or the number thirteen.

teenth. This is an especially dangerous combination of day and date. Friday, in itself, is supposed to be unlucky because that was the day on which Jesus Christ died, following the evening of the Last Supper with its thirteen guests at table.

Like the London group, the *National Committee of Thirteen* defied all the superstitions it could think of. Its members walked under ladders, lit three cigarettes on one match, broke mirrors, stepped on cracks, and marched into the paths of black cats. If a flight of stairs had thirteen steps, they wouldn't jump over the last step. If a building had a floor numbered thirteen, they wouldn't try to avoid it. This was sometimes hard to do, because many buildings "skipped" the number thirteen. The floor that came after the twelfth was called "fourteen."

The committee members made important business deals, got married, undertook long journeys, or moved from one dwelling to another on a Friday, all of which are considered very risky. And, of course, all thirteen members came together on Friday the thirteenth to share a meal. Amazingly, they seemed to survive just as well as anybody else!

Anti-superstition groups also like to remind us that there are thirteen doughnuts, rolls, or cookies in a "baker's dozen," thirteen weeks (roughly) in each season of the year; and thirteen stripes in the United States flag (for the thirteen original colonies).

The theme of thirteen is also carried out on the Great Seal of the United States. Both sides of this national medallion are engraved on the back of the one-dollar bill. If we turn a dollar bill over and examine it carefully, we'll see the face of the Great Seal — a circle with an eagle inside it — on the right. There are thirteen stripes on the eagle's shield and thirteen stars in the circlet above its head. In its left talon the eagle holds thirteen arrows and in its right talon an olive branch with thirteen leaves and thirteen berries on it. On the scroll caught in the eagle's beak is written the Latin motto *E Pluribus Unum,* which has thirteen letters in it. The motto's English translation — *Out of Many, One* — refers to the creation of the United States of America out of the thirteen colonies, as well as the many territories and states that followed.

The reverse side of the Great Seal can also be seen on the back of the one-dollar bill, to the left of the eagle. This side shows a pyramid made up of thirteen layers of stone. The pyramid is guarded by an eye enclosed in a triangle, set against a dazzling sunburst. This is the so-called Eye of Providence. It seems to be assuring us that there's luck in thirteen after all!

*

Money itself, of course, is something about which many people are superstitious. Almost everybody wants more of it. One way to increase our wealth, we are told, is to always fold our paper money toward us. If we fold it away from us, it will spend itself quickly.

Even coins can bring increased wealth. So we never give anyone a gift of a purse, wallet, or pocketbook without putting a coin inside it, on the theory that money helps money grow. It also never hurts to touch our money quickly at the sight of the new moon. As the moon waxes, or grows, so will our fortune.

A coin with the year of our birth on it is said to bring us good luck. This is also true for coins tossed into a fountain,

Which of us can pass a fountain without tossing in a coin or two to help our wishes come true?

wishing well, or other pool of water. Water is believed to be the source of all life and to have healing and purifying powers. So an offering of money may indeed bring us our wish.

"Heads you win, tails you lose." From the time of ancient Greece and Rome, coins were issued with the heads of powerful leaders on the front of them. The back of the coin was called the "tail." The winning side of the coin, in a toss, was the one with the ruler's head on it because of the belief that "might makes right."

Among ancient peoples, coins were of value even to the dead. The Greeks placed a coin called an "obol" in the mouth, or sometimes in the hand, of a dead person. According to Greek mythology, the soul was ferried across the River Styx to a place called "Hades" by a boatman known as "Charon." The obol would be demanded by Charon to pay for the ferry ride. It was believed that those souls without coins might have to wait for years to be carried across to Hades, the land of the dead, where they could rest at last.

The ancient Romans adopted many Greek customs and traditions, including this one. Like the Greeks, they would place the coin in the mouth, usually just beneath the tongue, of the dead person. Another practice through the ages has been to place coins on the closed eyelids of the dead. The reason, we are told, is that if the eyes were to open, the corpse might look around for someone to join it in death.

Clocks and watches are believed by some people to have an eerie connection with death. Many stories are told about clocks, especially grandfather clocks, that have stopped ticking for no mechanical reason at the very moment their owner died. Since clocks mark the minutes and hours of our lives, it's not surprising that we connect their ticking with our heartbeats and pulse beats. But usually a logical explanation can be found for why a clock might have run down. Perhaps the person who usually wound it had been ill for some time prior to dying and failed to care for the clock. Perhaps the worried family simply didn't notice the clock's silence until the moment when death struck. But, then again, maybe old clocks *are* very deep in their wisdom.

Lastly, have you ever been in a roomful of chattering people that suddenly went silent? For no apparent reason, all conversation came to a stop. There's an old superstition that says if you look at your watch, you'll find that it's either twenty minutes past the hour or twenty minutes to the hour.

The reason, many people say, is that Abraham Lincoln was shot to death at 8:20 in the evening as he sat in a theater in Washington, D.C., watching a play. So this is a moment on the clock when the specter of death, or perhaps the very ghost of Lincoln, intrudes on the living and causes a hush to descend. Further, we are told, most non-operating clocks displayed in jewelry stores have their hands arranged at 8:20 to commemorate the death of this famous president.

Unfortunately, the neatly put-together reason for this superstition doesn't quite hold up. History tells us that Lincoln was shot not at 8:20 in the evening but shortly after 10 P.M. He died, however, at 7:22 the following morning. So perhaps this partially explains the connection with the mysterious "twenty past the hour" silences.

As to the clocks and watches on display in stores, the placement of the large hand on the four (for twenty minutes past the hour) and the small hand on the eight is simply one way of showing off the face of the timepiece to best advantage. This practice among clockmakers, in fact, goes back to well before the assassination of President Lincoln.

The next time you are in a room that unexpectedly falls quiet, steal a look at the time. Suppose it *is* just twenty minutes past the hour. You will have to decide for yourself, won't you, whether this is mere coincidence or whether President Lincoln's ghost has wandered into your midst.

As a final caution among number superstitions, we are warned that we must never count the cars in a funeral procession. In this case, even seven is not a lucky number.

For the number of cars counted will be the same as the number of years we have left to live!

If you've gotten through the day without counting funeral cars, being handed a two-dollar bill, or finding yourself behind the eight ball, you can probably look forward to a good night's rest. As always in the world of superstition, however, there are a few possibly dangerous things you will have to watch out for as you prepare for sleep.

Can sleeping in the light of the full moon really cause our faces to swell and our minds to become "moonstruck"?

Don't Sleep in the Moonlight

New moon, new moon,
First time I see thee,
I hope before the week is out,
Something you'll have given me.

People have always been intrigued and mystified by the moon. From earliest times they watched the changes in this heavenly body and wondered about them. Every twenty-nine and a half days or so, the moon — which, incidentally, gives us the word *month* — would appear as a thin crescent in the sky. Gradually it would grow to a quarter moon, a half moon, and finally to a full circle of pearly, beaming light. Then, just as mysteriously, the moon would start to wane to a half, a quarter, a thinning crescent, until it disappeared almost entirely for a brief time.

This period is known as the "dark of the moon." Astronomers also call it the "new moon." But most of us think of the new moon as the first crescent of the growing moon.

We know today that the different "phases" of the moon are caused by the sun lighting up parts of its surface as it circles the Earth. But the old superstitions about the cycle of the moon are still with us.

Why do we make all sorts of wishes on the new moon? Because it seems so filled with promise. As the part of the moon that we can see grows in size, so we hope our good fortune will grow. We touch the silver coins in our pocket believing that the enlarging silvery glow in the sky will somehow increase our wealth.

There are some things to be careful of, though, in making a wish on the first crescent. We are told never to do so through a closed window. Looking at the moon through glass means that something will come between us and the good luck we are seeking. We may also glance at the moon over our *right* shoulder for luck but never over our left shoulder, for this is where evil is likely to lurk.

The luckiest new moon is said to be the first one of the new year. On the modern calendar, the new moon does not occur on January first. It appears in late January or early February. This is when the traditional Chinese New Year, with its dragon dances and firecrackers, is celebrated. The dragon of Chinese mythology is a terrifying-looking creature. It has fangs, claws, wings, and the scaly, slithery body of a serpent. But it is supposed to be a bringer of good fortune. The sharply sputtering and loudly booming firecrackers of the Chinese New Year celebration serve as an added powerful charm. They are set off to scare away evil spirits for an entire year to come!

Although the young crescent is said to be lucky, some of us become wary of the moon as it waxes, or grows, each month. For superstition tells us that the full moon can influence the mind. This is said to be especially true if we should sleep with the moon shining on our faces. Just as the moon

The fierce-looking dragon of the Chinese New Year, which celebrates the year's first new moon, is actually a bringer of good luck.

affects the tides, some say it can exert a "pull" on the human body. We may awake in the morning to find our faces swollen because the full moon has tried to "draw" us to it. Or we may look quite normal but will walk around all the next day feeling dazed, dreamy, and distracted. In other words, we are "moonstruck" or "moony."

Sleeping in the moonlight, some believe, can have even more serious effects. The words *lunatic, lunacy,* and *loony* all come from the Latin word for moon, which is *luna.* Can the full moon really bring on strange human behavior and even mental illness? Scientists say no. But many people point to the large number of fights, fires, accidents, crimes, and other violent acts that seem to take place at the time of the full moon. And who can ignore the tendency of dogs to bark at the moon? If animals react this way, isn't it just possible that humans may also become uneasy under the gaze of the full moon?

The period of the waning of the moon has its own set of superstitions. Some farmers believe that this is a good time to plant potatoes and other crops that grow underground. The plants won't be encouraged to seek the light during their first nights in the soil. It is also said that one should choose this time to cut corns, calluses, cuticles, and even hairs that one does not wish to grow again. There's no harm in trying out this idea. But it seems more than likely that these unwanted growths will return, just as the moon itself will grow to fullness once again!

*

Star light, star bright,
The first star I see tonight,
I wish I may, I wish I might,
Get the wish I wish tonight.

A belief that the distant stars are protective angels gives us the hope that they can make our wishes come true.

Like the new moon, the first star seen in the evening sky is said to bring luck and make wishes come true. This superstition may spring from the old belief that stars were either the souls of the dead or protective angels. A shooting, or falling, star was thought to be a human soul on its way to heaven. So wishing on one was particularly lucky, provided the wish was completed before the "star's" movement stopped.

We know today that the stars are really suns, and that "shooting stars" are not stars at all. They are falling meteors — particles or lumps of metallic or stony matter — that orbit our sun and take on a brilliant light from friction when they enter the Earth's atmosphere.

Even so, we tend to go on thinking of the stars as being connected in some supernatural way with our lives. We speak of a "star of destiny," one that will lead us to the fulfillment of our goals, and of "hitching our wagon to a star." If, on the other hand, our dreams don't work out, we say that "it wasn't in the stars," or that we are "star-crossed." In other words, we are ill-fated.

Those of us who believe in astrology feel that the positions of the sun, the moon, the stars, and the planets at the time of our birth can affect our entire lives. Scientists say there is no truth to the idea that these heavenly bodies can rule our destinies. Yet most of us like to look up our birth signs and see what they reveal about us. Often we say that somebody is a "perfect" Leo the Lion, or a "typical" Virgo. For their traits do surprisingly match the astrological description for that sign. And which of us can turn the pages of a newspaper without stopping to read our daily horoscope so we can find out "what's in the stars" for today?

*

Now I lay me down to sleep,
I pray the Lord my soul to keep;
If I should die before I wake,
I pray the Lord my soul to take.

These lines of verse are believed to be close to a thousand years old. Not surprisingly, there are many fears and superstitions connected with sleep. We spend about one third of our lives in this mysterious state, which has often been called the "brother of death."

Some people say that the first thing to do on going to bed is to make sure we sleep with our heads pointing north and our feet pointing south. This is because there is iron in the body that is attracted to the north and south poles of the Earth. We are told that if we sleep crosswise to the poles, in an east-west position, our sleep will be restless because the magnetic poles will be "pulling" at our hands and feet.

This "polar" theory sounds like it just might be the answer for restless sleepers. But unfortunately there isn't enough iron in the human body to react to the attraction of the Earth's poles. Also, before we go about rearranging our bedrooms, we should know that all sleepers are "restless." Nobody sleeps "like a log." Tests have proved that it is perfectly normal for us to change our position dozens of times during the night.

Sleeping "like a top" is also pretty unnatural. We don't spin around as we sleep. In fact, it's believed that this expression comes from the French word *taupe*. A *taupe* is a mole. This small burrowing animal lives underground, is almost blind, and appears to sleep a lot because it is seldom seen scampering about. Also, our sense of sight is the first one we lose as we begin to drop off to sleep.

Do we sleep better before midnight than we do after midnight? Many people believe this is so. But it isn't necessarily true. More likely it's just a good reason to get us to go to bed earlier so we'll be less unwilling to get up in the morning. Superstition, of course, would tell us that midnight is the "witching hour," a time when ghosts and unruly spirits may walk the earth and make us wakeful. So the only peaceful sleep we can be sure of is the sleep we get before the clock strikes twelve.

What about the idea that sleeping on our right side is better because our heart is on our left side and can be injured by extra weight pressing on it? This, too, is a fallacy. Actually the heart is in almost the middle of the chest. Perhaps this belief was dictated by the old superstition that right is better than left.

Another dangerous practice is said to be that of sleeping with a younger or weaker person, such as a small child. The younger person is believed to mysteriously "draw" strength from the older person and weaken him or her. The real reason why one would probably wake up feeling "weak" or tired is that a night beside a whimpering baby or a tiny kicking child isn't likely to be very restful in the first place!

"Night air is bad for you." This is an old-time warning against opening a window in a room where one is sleeping. The fear of night breezes is probably connected with the disease malaria, which was once widespread and is carried by mosquitoes that bite their victims mainly at night. The word *malaria* is from the Italian *mal' aria,* or "bad air," because the foul-smelling swamps where the mosquitoes breed were originally thought to be the direct cause of the disease. In most cases, however, a little fresh air in a room seems to help us sleep better.

On the other hand, open windows probably aren't a very good idea for people who are apt to walk in their sleep. Sleepwalking is a strange condition that most often occurs in childhood. Sleepwalkers seem to be unconscious of what they are doing as they get out of bed and walk around a room, a house, or even out of doors. Amazingly they seem to overcome obstacles and seldom hurt themselves. But it isn't true that they lead a charmed life while sleepwalking.

As sleep sometimes appears similar to death, superstitious people believe that the soul may leave the body during both ordinary sleep and sleepwalking. Therefore, they say, a sleepwalker must never be wakened suddenly, even when danger is near. The soul may not have time to return to the body, and the person will die.

Doctors, however, tell us that there is no harm in waking a sleepwalker abruptly. Furthermore, we may not have much choice, especially if the sleepwalker is about to step off a busy curbside or over the edge of a steep cliff!

*

Sleepwalkers, it is thought, are acting out their dreams, which they may or may not remember the next morning. But what about the dreams that the rest of us have? Scientists say that everybody has dreams, probably four to six of them a night. But we remember only some of them. People who say they never dream probably just don't remember any of the images, thoughts, or feelings they experienced in their sleep.

There are many theories as to what causes our dreams and what they mean. Some people say that the foods we eat before bed can affect our dreams. Dreaming of picking blackberries, for example, is supposed to forewarn sickness. Could dreaming of food result from having eaten too much

Sleepwalkers, an old superstition says, must never be awakened suddenly for fear that their souls will flee their bodies.

of a particular treat before going to sleep, one that has already begun to give us a queasy stomach?

We are also told that indigestion or overexcitement can give us nightmares. The "mare" that causes our frightful and terrifying dreams is said to be an evil spirit that is trying to "crush" us.

A dream of muddy water is considered a bad dream because it means trouble or death. Perhaps this has to do with the superstition that not seeing our reflection in a pool or mirror means that our soul has fled. And dreaming of snakes is supposed to mean you have an enemy. Or is this just another way of seeing a "snake in the grass"?

Do we dream in color? Many of us report that we do. People who see colors vividly in their dreams are said to do so because they have a more strongly developed color sense. Color-blind people may well dream in shades of gray like those seen on a black-and-white television screen.

There are many superstitions associated with colors, in both our waking and sleeping life. Red is a symbol of danger, violence, and sin, probably because it is the color of blood and fire. We speak of "seeing red" when we become angry. And bullfighters wave a red cape at a bull to irritate it. Bulls do tend to charge at a swirling cape but not because it is red, for bulls are color-blind! It is the movement of the cloth that infuriates them.

Red-haired people, especially women, are the victims of a prejudice that says they are hot-tempered and overly excitable. This is as unfair as saying that all green-eyed people are jealous and not to be trusted. Both red-haired and green-eyed people are probably frowned on by superstition because, like left-handed people, they are in the minority.

Blue-eyed people, on the other hand, are thought to be sincere and truthful. We speak of someone who is highly trustworthy as being "true blue," for this is the color of the "heavens" in fair weather. Blue is also a reward for excellence, which is why a blue ribbon is often presented as a prize.

Because of its resemblance to the sky, blue is thought to be a lucky color, one that will drive away evil. Brides traditionally wear:

> Something old, something new,
> Something borrowed, something blue.

The "something old" in the verse is supposed to be an article that has brought good luck in the past. The "something new" is a symbol of hope for the future. The "something borrowed" is intended to add the good luck of a well-wisher to the bride's costume. And the "something blue" is to ensure that wicked spirits won't spoil the wedding day or the marriage itself.

Blue is also the color that distinguishes baby boys from baby girls. Throughout history, certain peoples have always considered sons more valuable than daughters. So it isn't surprising that, in more recent times, the "lucky" color, blue, was assigned to boys. Pink, as the color for girls, is believed to have been chosen as an afterthought.

Black is associated with death in many parts of the world. But did you know that the use of black clothing and dark veils as a sign of mourning actually comes from a desire to make ourselves invisible? According to superstition, death hovered for some time around the relatives and friends of one of its victims. They themselves were in danger of being chosen for the grave. So they dressed in dark colors to try to keep from being seen. The mourning veil came to serve another purpose for women. It concealed the faces of those whose eyes were red and swollen from weeping — and also the faces of those who hadn't shed a single tear of sorrow!

Not all cultures, though, have connected black with mourning. For Chinese and other Asians, white is traditionally the color of death and of the mourner's clothing. Among other peoples, yellow, the color of fading plants, commemorates the dead.

If colors follow you into your dreams, so can superstition. But does dreaming of fire and blood really mean anger or violence? Is a dream of blue skies a sign of peace and happiness? Does a dream of shadowy black figures signify death? Do our dreams reflect the past, or do they foretell the future? Or are they simply a jumble of images and reactions based in part on what we watched on television last night!

Perhaps Jonathan Swift, the author of *Gulliver's Travels*, best summed up the subject of dreams nearly three hundred years ago when he wrote:

> [Dreams] are mere productions of the brain,
> And fools consult interpreters in vain.

*

A final superstition about sleeping tells us that if we have the same dream three nights in a row, it will come true. Here we are again, involved with the lucky — or not-so-lucky — number three. So if our dream *is* going to become a reality, we'd better make sure to have a good one!

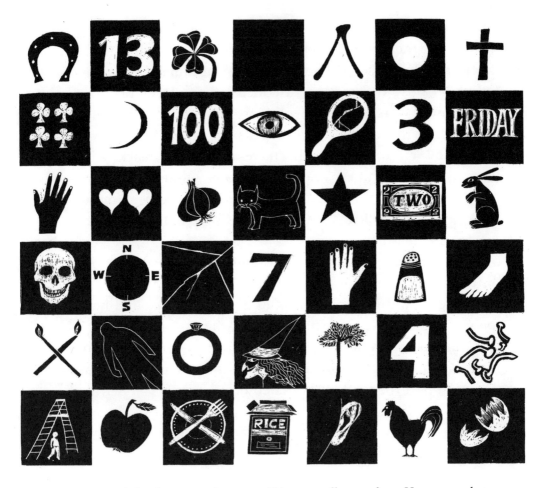

The symbols of our everyday superstitions are all around us. How many do we ignore? How many are we wary of?

But what if we don't? How far should we let superstition take us? As we've seen, the beginnings of most superstitions can be quite easily explained. They were based on ignorance, fear, prejudice — and above all on hope.

Life itself was a mystery. It was too awesome to be lived without some kind of magic. People needed to believe there were charms and spells that would work against the terrors of both the known and the unknown.

What about today? Surely we don't think that evil spirits are going to take away the world's supply of salt if we tip over a few grains by accident. Surely we don't believe that the wooden chair or table we knock on is the home of an ancient god. Surely we aren't going to send our mothers to an early grave if we step on a crack in the sidewalk.

And yet . . . And yet . . . Where did I leave my rabbit's foot? Why did I put on my left shoe first this morning? Did I just hear myself *humming a tune before breakfast*?

Bibliography

Ashley, Leonard R. N., *The Wonderful World of Superstition, Prophecy, and Luck.* New York: Dembner Books, 1984.

Brasch, R., *How Did It Begin? Customs and Superstitions and Their Romantic Origins.* New York: David McKay, 1965.

Brown, Raymond Lamont, *A Book of Superstitions.* New York: Taplinger, 1970.

de Lys, Claudia, *A Treasury of American Superstitions.* New York: Philosophical Library, 1948.

Ferm, Virgilius, *A Brief Dictionary of American Superstitions.* New York: Philosophical Library, 1959.

Jobes, Gertrude, *Dictionary of Mythology, Folklore, and Symbols.* New York: Scarecrow Press, 1962.

Opie, Iona and Peter, *The Lore and Language of Schoolchildren.* London: Oxford University Press, 1959.

Radford, E. and M. A., *Encyclopaedia of Superstitions.* Edited and revised by Christina Hole. Chester Springs, Pa.: Dufour, 1961.

Index